Mine, Mine, Mine
Said the Porcupine

'Mine, Mine, Mine Said the Porcupine'
An original concept by Alex English
© Alex English

Illustrated by Emma Levey

Published by MAVERICK ARTS PUBLISHING LTD

Studio 3A, City Business Centre, 6 Brighton Road,

Horsham, West Sussex, RH13 5BB

© Maverick Arts Publishing Limited July 2017

+44 (0)1403 256941

A CIP catalogue record for this book is available at the British Library.

ISBN 978-1-84886-296-8

Maverick
arts publishing
www.maverickbooks.co.uk

Blue

This book is rated as: Blue Band (Guided Reading)
The original picture book text for this story has been modified by the author to be an early reader.

Mine, Mine, Mine
Said the Porcupine

by **Alex English**
Illustrated by **Emma Levey**

A porcupine went to see Sam.

"Good!" said Sam.

"You can play with me!"

"Shall we play with this?" said Sam.

"No, that is MINE!" said the porcupine.

"Shall we play rockets?" said Sam.

"No, that rocket is mine!"

said the porcupine.

"There are lots of things we can play!"

said Sam.

"Or we can do a painting!" said Sam.

But the porcupine just said, "Mine!"

"MINE!"

"MINE!"

"MINE!"

Sam said, "All right. I will not play

with you. I will play in the land of Kaboo."

The land of Kaboo was fun.

Sam had fun jumping and running
and skidding.

He sang as he swung in the trees.

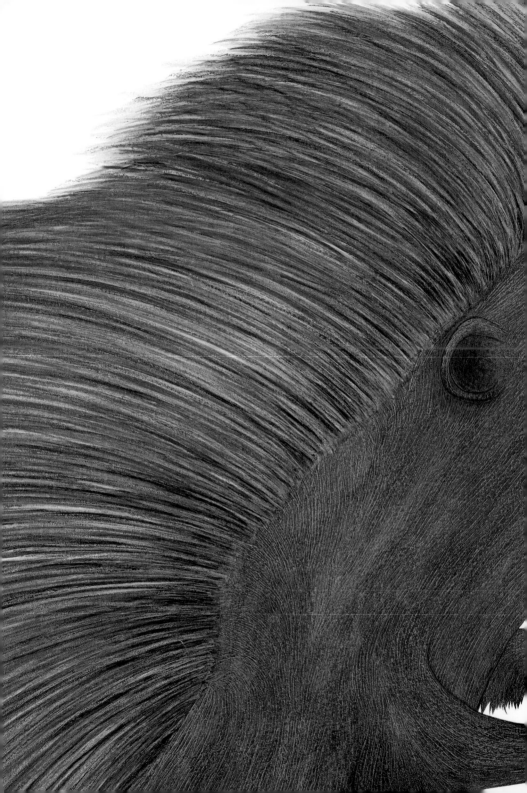

"Can I play too?" said the porcupine.

"Please?"

"Yes," said Sam. "Just grab my hand."

Sam and the porcupine ran off to play.

"Now you can be my best friend," said Sam.

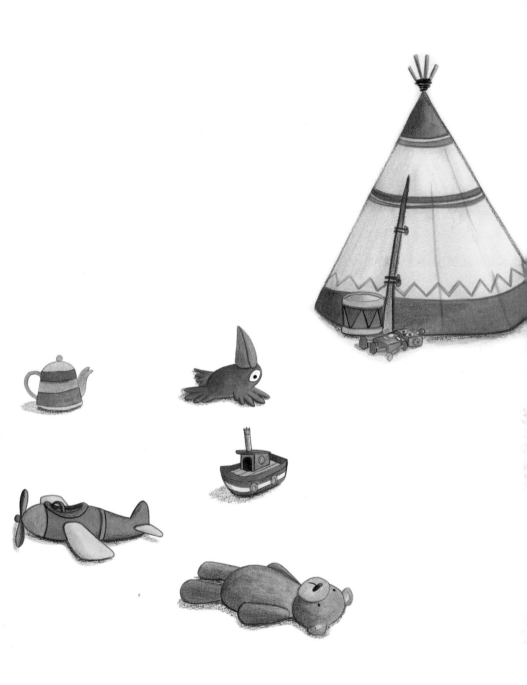

"And you can be mine,"

said the porcupine.

Quiz

1. Who comes to Sam's house?
a) A dog
b) A porcupine
c) A cat

2. What does the porcupine do?
a) He takes Sam's toys
b) He runs away
c) He jumps on Sam's rocket

3. But the porcupine just said...?
a) "Mine!"
b) "Yuck!"
c) "Bang!"

4. Sam goes to the land of _____?

a) Rockets

b) Porcupines

c) Kaboo

5. Why can Sam and the porcupine play at the end?

a) They sing together

b) Sam says "mine!"

c) The porcupine says, "please."

Turn over for answers

Book Bands for Guided Reading

The Institute of Education book banding system is a scale of colours that reflects the various levels of reading difficulty. The bands are assigned by taking into account the content, the language style, the layout and phonics.

Maverick Early Readers are a bright, attractive range of books covering the pink to purple bands. All of these books have been book banded for guided reading to the industry standard and edited by a leading educational consultant.

For more titles visit:
www.maverickbooks.co.uk/early-readers

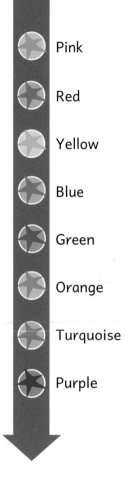

Pink

Red

Yellow

Blue

Green

Orange

Turquoise

Purple

Book Band Blue

Fast Fox and Slow Snail	978-1-84886-295-1
Mine, Mine, Mine Said the Porcupine	978-1-84886-296-8
The Smart Hat	978-1-84886-294-4
Strictly No Crocs	978-1-84886-240-1
Bibble and the Bubbles	978-1-84886-224-1

Quiz Answers: 1b, 2a, 3a, 4c, 5c